LETTERS HOME from EGYPT

Marcia S. Gresko

BLACKBIRCH PRESS, INC.

WOODBRIDGE, CONNECTICUT

Published by Blackbirch Press, Inc.
260 Amity Road
Woodbridge, CT 06525

©1999 by Blackbirch Press, Inc.
First Edition

e-mail: staff@blackbirch.com
Web site: www.blackbirch.com

Printed in Singapore

10 9 8 7 6 5 4 3 2 1

Photo Credits

Cover and title page: ©Corel Corporation; pages 6 (left), 7, 13 (left), 14, 16, 17: ©Egyptian Tourist Authority; pages 6 (right), 8-11, 18-27, 29, 31: ©Corel Corporation; page 12: ©George Mobley/National Geographic; page 13: ©National Geographic Image Collection; page 15: ©Winfield Parks/National Geographic; page 28: ©Thomas J. Abercrombie/National Geographic; page 30: David S. Boyle/National Geographic.

Library of Congress Cataloging-in-Publication Data

Gresko, Marcia S.
Egypt / by Marcia S. Gresko.
    p.   cm. — (Letters home from . . .)
Includes bibliographical references and index.
Summary: Describes some of the sights and experiences on a trip to Egypt, including visits to Cairo, Giza, Alexandria, Luxor, and Thebes.
ISBN 1-56711-401-6
1. Egypt—Description and travel. Juvenile literature. 2. Gresko, Marcia S.—Journeys— Egypt Juvenile literature. [1. Egypt—Description and travel.] I. Title. II. Series.
DT56.2.G74 1999   99-23118
916.204'55—dc21   CIP

TABLE OF CONTENTS

Arrival in . . .

Cairo

It was a frosty, winter day at home when we boarded the plane for Egypt. But when we arrived in Cairo, the capital city, I was glad I'd packed sunglasses and suntan lotion! Egypt's winters are mild and sunny. Its summers are scorching. There are only two seasons in Egypt.

Our guide said visiting Egypt is really like visiting two continents! Most of the country is in the northeastern corner of Africa, but Egypt's Sinai Peninsula is part of Asia. It's also like hopping into a time machine. Everywhere there are spectacular reminders that Egyptian civilization has been around a long time—about 5,000 years.

Temples and tombs, mosques and mummies, Egypt is full of mysteries waiting to be explored!

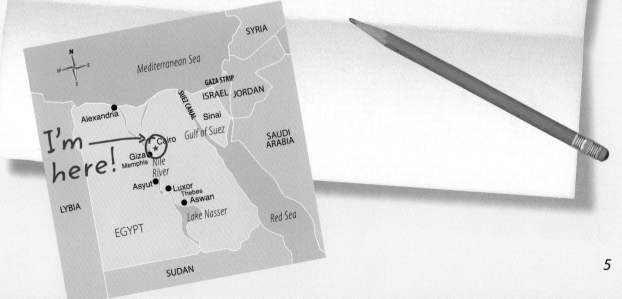

I'm here!

SYRIA

Mediterranean Sea

GAZA STRIP
ISRAEL JORDAN

SUEZ CANAL

Alexandria
Sinai

Cairo
Gulf of Suez

SAUDI
ARABIA

Giza
Memphis   Nile
River

Asyut
Luxor
Thebes
Aswan

LYBIA

Lake Nasser

Red Sea

EGYPT

SUDAN

Modern Cairo

Everywhere we went, Cairo was packed with people! More than 10 million people of all shapes, sizes, and colors live in Cairo. It's not only the largest city in Egypt, it's the largest city in Africa!

Cairo sprawls across the Nile River and includes two islands in its middle. It's really a mix of old and new. The newer sections have skyscrapers, glittering shops, and all the modern hotels. (Our hotel is here, too.) There are grand museums, government buildings, and universities. Cairo is Egypt's center of business and government, culture, and education.

Kids on a felucca (sailboat)

Modern Cairo, from the west

6

Downtown Cairo

Nile in Cairo

Yesterday we wandered the Khan al Kahlili Market, one of the largest bazaars in the world. You can find almost anything there. Fabrics, perfumes, leather goods, jewelry, and woodwork.

Today we explored the area south of the market where the city's most important Islamic sites are located. It's easy to get lost there! The maze of streets is crowded with donkeys and buses, shops and mosques, people and pushcarts.

After a tasty pita bread sandwich filled with roasted lamb, or shawarma, we headed further south to the very oldest part of Cairo. We wanted to see the ancient Roman fort and many important Coptic Christian churches that are located there.

7

Ancient Cairo

According to the guidebook, four important cities have been built over the centuries where present-day Cairo now stands!

Memphis, the first capital of ancient Egypt, was founded nearby about 5,000 years ago. It was the country's capital during the Old Kingdom—that's the time when the great pyramids were built. Historians who study ancient Egypt divide the country's earliest history into three major time periods— the Old Kingdom, the Middle Kingdom, and the New Kingdom.

A Roman fortress city called Babylon also stood here. The Roman Empire ruled Egypt for centuries.

Then, about 1,300 years ago, Arab invaders from the east set up Egypt's first Arab capital here. This capital was called Fustat.

Khufu Pyramid

Great pyramids

About 300 years later, Arab tribes from northern Africa conquered the country and built a new capital, Al Qahirah, which means "victorious city." That's where the name Cairo comes from.

The city was later expanded by the famous warrior, Saladin. You can see his crest, the eagle, on the Egyptian flag. Saladin built the massive palace fort, called the Citadel. Egypt's rulers governed from the Citadel for about 700 years.

Cairo's ancient beginnings are everywhere. And, as we watched the sun set over the distant pyramids, it was easy to see why the city has been called "the Mother of the World."

Giza

The three giant pyramids of Giza, just west of Cairo, are an amazing sight! The largest and oldest of the three pyramids is the Great Pyramid. It was built as the grand tomb of King Khufu. It's 450 feet high—nearly as tall as a 40-story skyscraper. Its base covers seven city blocks. You could fit 10 football fields in it! About 2.5 million limestone blocks were used to build the pyramid. It is estimated that 100,000 men worked in 3-month shifts for 20 years to complete it.

Khufu's son Khafre and the pharaoh Menkaure built the other two pyramids. The Great Sphinx, a huge stone lion with the head of a man, guards the way to Khafre's pyramid. Historians think it represents King Khafre himself. Our guide said that its missing nose and beard were shot off during target practice by soldiers hundreds of years ago.

The Great Sphinx

Khafre Pyramid

Memphis

We took a train 15 miles south of Cairo to Memphis, Egypt's very first capital city. The city was founded by Menes, the first king of Egypt. King Menes united Upper and Lower Egypt to create the world's first national government.

There wasn't much left of ancient Memphis to see, but the nearby Saqqara was amazing. Bustling Memphis buried its pharaohs, nobles, and even its sacred bulls in tombs and pyramids here! The grandest is the Step Pyramid, the first pyramid ever built. When it was completed for King Djoser, more than 4,500 years ago, it was the largest stone structure in the world. Its 6 gigantic steps rise about 200 feet high and were supposed to be the stairway by which the dead pharaoh would reach the sun god in the sky.

Stonecutters, Saqqara

Sphinx of Memphis

Alexandria

We're spending the weekend in the city of Alexandria, on the Mediterranean Sea. Alexandria is Egypt's chief port and its second-largest city.

During our bus ride north, our driver told us the city's history.

When the young military genius, Alexander the Great of Greece, conquered Egypt, he built a new capital city, Alexandria. Before he died, Alexander gave Egypt to one of his best generals, Ptolemy.

The dynasty Ptolemy founded, known as the Ptolemies, ruled Egypt for 300 years. During that time, Alexandria became a center of Greek culture. Scientists, mathematicians, poets, historians, geographers, and engineers studied and worked here. The city became famous for its great library and for the world's first lighthouse, the 400-foot-tall Pharos of Alexandria. Along with the pyramids, the lighthouse was one of the Seven Wonders of the Ancient World.

Souk (market)

Roman amphitheater

Alexandria

The Ptolemies ruled Egypt until the Romans captured it from the famous Queen Cleopatra. The white marble terraces of the Roman amphitheater reminded us that Alexandria was once an important Roman port.

Today, most visitors are tourists like us, or Egyptians escaping the country's scorching summer weather. Cool, fresh sea breezes, busy markets, and historic sites make Alexandria the perfect vacation spot!

13

Daily Life

Like Cairo, Alexandria was packed with people. About half of all Egyptians live in cities, making their homes in everything from luxury apartments to slums and even cemeteries!

As we boarded the bus to return to Cairo this morning, people were hurrying to their jobs in offices, shops, factories, or street bazaars. Most wore western-style clothes, but some men still wore traditional loose-fitting robes.

We got back to Cairo just as the muezzin, or prayer announcer, was chanting the call to evening prayers. No matter where you are in Egypt—city or village—everyone stops. In the mosques, shops, or fields, strict Muslims kneel and pray.

Camel herd

Muslims at Mosque

Ramadan

Most Egyptians are Muslims, followers of Islam. Muhammad was the founder of Islam. Muslims believe he was the prophet, or messenger, of God who they call Allah. Muhammad's teachings were written down in the holy book called the Koran. Ramadan is Islam's most important holiday. It celebrates Muhammad receiving the Koran from God. Ramadan lasts a whole month! During that time Muslims fast from sunrise to sunset and then feast and party into the night.

Suez Canal

Today we traveled 140 miles east from Cairo to Port Said. Port Said is on the Mediterranean Sea at the northern entrance of the Suez Canal.

As we watched the huge cargo ships and great tankers lining up to pass through the canal's entrance, our guide explained that the Suez Canal connects the Mediterranean Sea to the Red Sea. The human-made canal was built more than 100 years ago by a partnership between the countries of France and Great Britain. It is the quickest sea route between Europe and the Middle and Far East. Ships take about 15 hours to cruise their way through the 118-mile-long, 64-foot deep canal. But, it cuts 6,000 miles off the journey between Europe and Asia. About 17,000 ships pass through it each year. It's the busiest stretch of waterway in the world!

Suez canal

Sinai

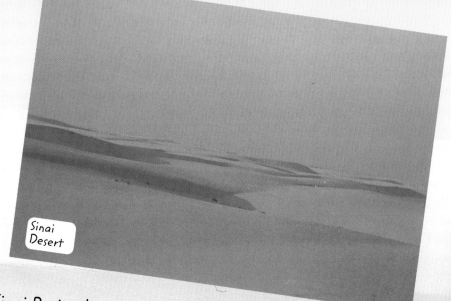

Sinai Desert

Our trip to the Sinai Peninsula took us to a different continent. Most of Egypt is in Africa. But once our ferry crossed the Suez Canal, we were in Asia! Because of its location, the Sinai Peninsula has been used like a land bridge between Asia and Africa. Many battles have been fought to control it.

The scenery outside our window was mostly barren desert and rocky mountains. But, there are also coastal resorts where you can explore the Red Sea's colorful coral reefs.

According to the guidebook, the Sinai Peninsula is an ancient land of miracles and holy places. Many believe it is here that God spoke to Moses from a burning bush, where the waters of the Red Sea were parted, and where the Ten Commandments were delivered.

Bedouins

No matter where we go in Egypt, there are camels! But I didn't get to ride one until today.

We took a day trip to a small Bedouin village at an oasis a few miles from our hotel. Ibrahim, the Bedouin guide who led our group, lived there. He explained that like many Bedouin families, he and his family used to live a nomadic, or wandering, lifestyle. They would follow their herds of camels, goats, and sheep to new grazing areas, pitching

Bedouin elder

Bedouin woman carrying baby

Bedouin camp

Bedouin on an Arabian horse

their tents wherever there was grass and water. They made their living from the milk and meat of their animals, and by selling handicrafts like rugs or jewelry. Now he and his family are settled in the village. They earn a living by farming dates, raising livestock, and leading tourists like us on camel safaris.

According to Ibrahim, camels are the perfect desert transportation. There are still more camel trails than roads in the Sinai! Camels have been nicknamed the "ships of the desert" because they can cross oceans of sand carrying heavy loads. And even though they store fat, not water, in their humps, they can go for days or even weeks without drinking. But watch out, a thirsty camel can drink 25 gallons (400 glasses) of water without stopping!

Nile River

We're spending a few days on a cruise boat anchored in Luxor. Then we're taking a trip up the Nile to Aswan.

The Nile River is the longest river in the world! It rises near the equator in Africa, and flows for 4,145 miles into the Mediterranean Sea.

Without the Nile, Egypt would be one big desert. Ancient Egyptians called their land Kemet, which meant "black land" for the rich, dark soil of the Nile River valley. They called the surrounding desert Deshret or "red land".

Nile River

Irrigation canal

Every year they would wait for the river to flood its banks and spread the life-giving silt, or mud, and water over the Nile Valley. Farmers would then plant their crops in the fertile soil.

Today the Nile Delta and the Nile Valley are still one of the world's best farming regions. Most of Egypt's people live in these two areas.

Egypt's wildlife is also centered around the Nile. Temple scenes of hippos, gazelles, crocodiles, wildcats, and ostriches show that these animals were once plentiful. But, overpopulation of the surrounding area has made wildlife rare. Our guide said that we'd see lots of birds and maybe a crocodile.

Karnak

Karnak Temple's evening sound-and-light show was awesome! But the religious ceremonies and rituals that took place here thousands of years ago were even grander.

Ancient Egyptians worshipped hundreds of gods and goddesses who they believed were responsible for everything from sickness to floods. Carvings on the walls and columns of the temple showed many of them. Some took the form of humans or animals. Many had human bodies and animal heads. The main god was the hawk-headed sun god, Re. The most important goddess was the great mother-goddess, Isis. Each town, family, and profession had its own special gods, too.

Karnak

Karnak

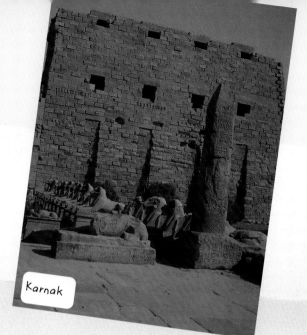

Karnak

The most important gods were worshipped in huge temples. Karnak, built in honor of Amun-Re, was Egypt's largest temple. Its Great Hall was like a forest of more than 130 carved stone columns, each taller than a 6-story building.

In ancient times, powerful priests and priestesses looked after the temples and served the gods who were honored there. Each day they would wash, dress, and make lavish food offerings to a statue of the god. Sometimes these statues would be displayed during special festival celebrations. Farms and craft workshops, which were part of the temple complex, provided for all the gods' needs from food to jewelry!

Luxor

Visiting Luxor was like going to a giant outdoor museum! The city is built on and around the ancient city of Thebes.

Many pharaohs left their mark on Luxor. The pictures carved into the walls, ceilings, and columns of the Temple of Luxor are like a history book. The symbols recorded the story of the pharaohs, their words and deeds, and the great events that happened during their rule.

Our guide explained that the ancient Egyptians used hieroglyphics (picture writing) for about 3,000 years. Some symbols stood for objects.

Temple of Luxor

Pictures in stone

Luxor courtyard

For example, wavy lines represented water. A picture could also stand for an idea. Walking feet meant a journey, a mouth meant a speech. Some hieroglyphs represented sounds just like the letters in the alphabet.

There were more than 700 commonly used hieroglyphs, mostly plants, animals, people, and objects. Writing was done by highly trained men called scribes. Most Egyptians could not read or write, and scribes were highly respected. A scribe named Horemheb even became a pharaoh!

When writing and record-keeping became more important, the Egyptians invented a paper-like material they called papyrus. Our word "paper" comes from that word.

Thebes

This morning we took a ferry to visit the Valley of the Kings. When Thebes was the capital of the New Kingdom, powerful pharaohs like Ramses II built a huge necropolis (city of the dead) on the Nile's west bank.

As we crossed the river, our guide reminded us that ancient Egyptians believed in life after death. After death, the body was made into a mummy to keep it from decaying. This way a dead person's spirit could recognize it and bring it to life in the next world.

Proper mummification took about 70 days. First, the internal organs were removed. Some were preserved in jars to be buried with the person. The

Cleopatra with double cobras

Ramses II in form of Horus

Sphinxes

Tutankhamen's funerary mask

heart, which the Egyptians thought controlled the body, was left in place. But the brain was removed and thrown away! The empty body was filled with cloth pads and packed in special salt crystals until it dried out. Then it was wrapped in layers of linen. Magic charms were often placed in the layers to protect it. Mummies were placed in coffins of wood or stone and then placed in burial chambers inside grand tombs.

The tombs, tunneled into the valley walls, once held great riches. Objects for the pharaoh's afterlife, from thrones and chariots to games and food, were buried with him. But tomb robbers had stolen them all until the sealed tomb of Tutankhamen was discovered. More than 5,000 treasures were rescued from his tomb. His mummy was left where it was buried more than 3,000 years ago.

Thebes

Today we saw more sights on the west bank of the Nile. My favorites were the Tombs of the Nobles and the Temple of Hatshepsut.

The Tombs of the Nobles were where New Kingdom nobles, priests, and important officials were buried. The paintings on the walls showed us how people lived. There were scenes of everyday life—farming, fishing, and hunting.

The Temple of Hatshepsut was carved right into the solid stone mountainside. Hatshepsut was Egypt's only female pharaoh. When her husband died, she was supposed to rule until her stepson grew up. Instead, she wore men's clothing and the false gold beard of the king, and had herself crowned pharaoh! She ruled for more than 20 years.

Wall painting of Nile River scene

Idfu and Esna Temples

Our boat began its 135-mile cruise down the Nile to Aswan yesterday.

We stopped to visit the ruins of three temples on the way. These temples were much newer than those at Luxor—less than 2,000 years old! They were built by rulers who conquered Egypt—the Greeks and the Romans. Because they ruled from distant Alexandria, the temples were important symbols of the new rulers in this part of Egypt.

Our first stop was 30 miles south of Luxor at the Temple of Khnum at Esna. It was dedicated to the ram-headed god who Egyptians believed created man on a potter's wheel.

Further south was the Temple of Horus in Idfu. According to legend, it stands on the site where two gods fought to the death.

Ancient temple

Ancient columns

Aswan

Our cruise boat arrived in Aswan, Egypt's southernmost city, a few days ago. Yesterday we took a tour of two amazing landmarks. Five miles south of Aswan is the Aswan High Dam. What a sight! The enormous 2.5-mile-long, 300-foot-high dam has 17 times more building material in it than the Great Pyramid of Khufu at Giza! It took 30,000 men 10 years to complete it. Behind the dam is Lake Nasser, the largest human-made lake in the world.

Our second stop was further south at the gigantic Temples of Abu Simbel. As we stared at the statues of Ramses II, each as tall as a five-story building, our guide told us the incredible story of their rescue. Cut into a mountainside more than 3,000 years ago, the temples were threatened with

Aswan Dam

Nubian village

Nubian boat boy

drowning in Lake Nasser. Thousands of engineers and workers from all over the world worked together to move them stone by stone to a specially built mountain where they were reassembled.

Today we boarded a felucca, a traditional Nile sailboat. Our friendly boat captain and his son were Nubians. They're descendants of an ancient people of African and Arab ancestry. Many Nubians lost their homes when the Aswan High Dam was built. Some, like our captain, moved north and settled in villages on the islands around Aswan.

Glossary

Bazaar a street market.

Civilization an advanced stage of human organization, technology, and culture.

Dynasty a family who rules a country.

Fertile a condition of land that is good for growing crops.

Pharaoh title of the ancient kings of Egypt.

Prophet a person who speaks, or claims to speak, from God.

Scorching extremely hot.

Slum overcrowded, poor, and neglected area of housing in a town or city.

Tomb a grave, room, or building for holding a dead body.

For More Information

Books

Bickman, Connie. *Egypt* (Through the Eyes of Children). Minneapolis, MN: Abdo & Daughters, 1996.

Flint, David. *Egypt* (On the Map). Chatham, NJ: Raintree/Steck Vaughn, 1994.

Steele, Philip. *The Best Book of Mummies*. Las Vegas, NV: Kingfisher Books, 1998.

Web Sites

Tour Egypt

See Egypt on an adventure safari by air, land, or water— www.touregypt.net/wildegypt.

Pyramids—The Inside Story

Explore the pyramids and find out who built them— www.pbs.org/wgbh/nova/pyramid.

Index